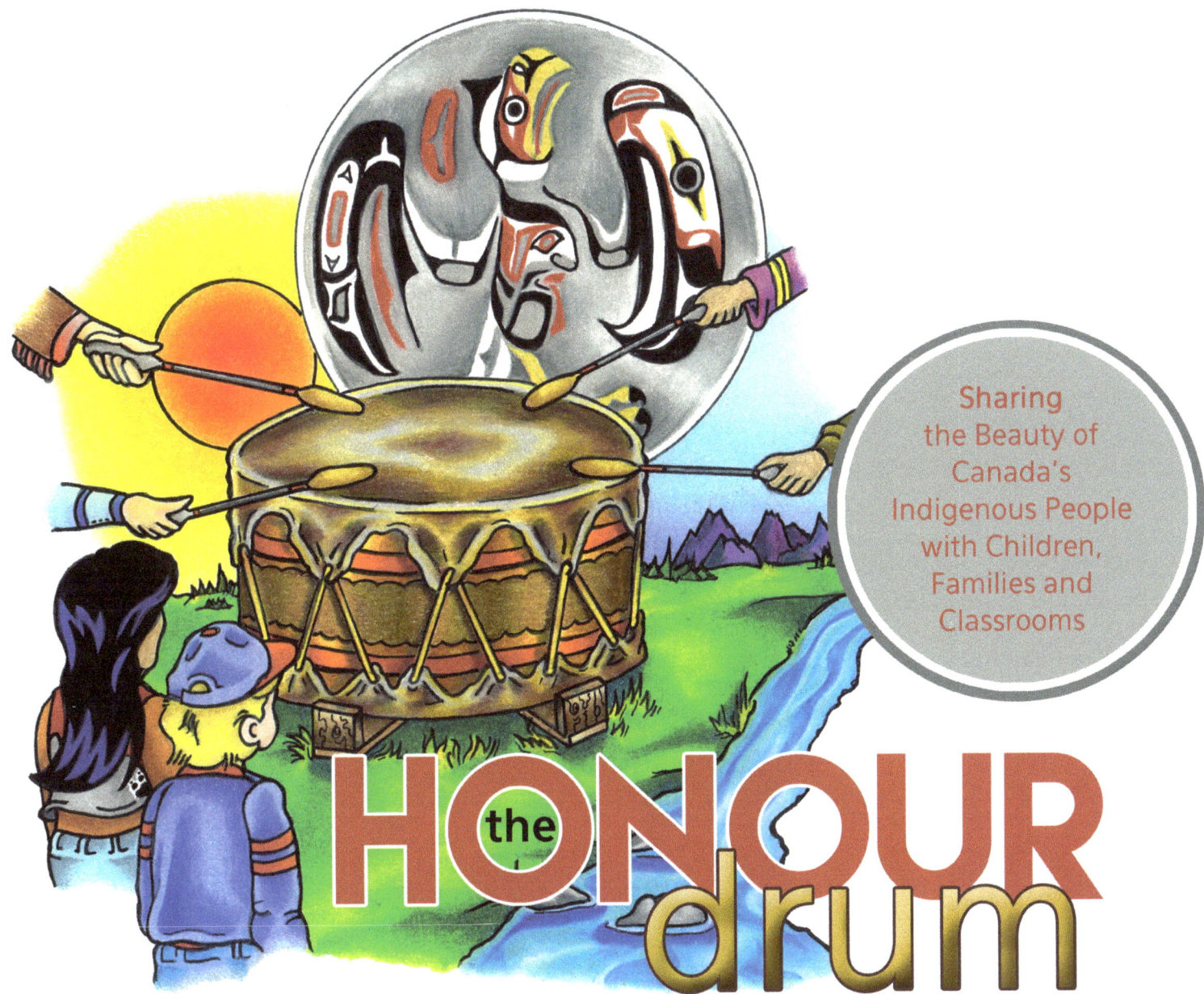

Sharing the Beauty of Canada's Indigenous People with Children, Families and Classrooms

the HONOUR drum

WRITTEN BY CHERYL BEAR AND TIM HUFF
PARENT AND TEACHER DISCUSSION GUIDE BY CHERYL BEAR
ILLUSTRATED BY TIM HUFF

The Honour Drum: Sharing the Beauty of Canada's Indigenous People with Children, Families and Classrooms
Copyright ©2016 Tim Huff and Cheryl Bear
2nd printing 2023
All rights reserved

ISBN 978-1-998815-12-8 hard cover
ISBN 978-1-927355-65-7 EPUB

Published by:
Castle Quay Books
Burlington, Ontario and Tequesta, Florida
Tel: (416) 573-3249
E-mail: info@castlequaybooks.com   www.castlequaybooks.com

Edited by Marina Hofman Willard
Cover design and inside layout by Burst Impressions

Library and Archives Canada Cataloguing in Publication

Bear, Cheryl, author
    The honour drum : sharing the beauty of Canada's indigenous
people with children, families and classrooms / written by Cheryl Bear
and Tim Huff ; parent and teacher discussion guide by Cheryl Bear
; illustrated by Tim Huff ; forewords by Ray Aldred and Steve Bell.

(Compassion series)
ISBN 978-1-998815-12-8 (hardcover)

    1. Native peoples--Canada--Juvenile literature. I. Huff, Tim,
1964-, author, illustrator II. Title.

E78.C2B43 2016   j971.004'97   C2016-904539-0

CASTLE QUAY BOOKS

Foreword by Ray Aldred

DEAR READER,

THE DRUM IS THE PLACE WHERE ALL OF OUR RELATIVES GATHER. THIS BOOK SEEKS TO HONOUR THE RELATIONSHIPS that make up our lives. The rhythm of the drum and rhythm of this book help draw out the dance that is within all of creation. The authors of this book have done a marvellous job of helping lead a community to find and affirm the dance that lies at the heart of each person, the dance that Creator has put into all things.

The children keep the old people alive because they bring healing, just as the south wind brings healing in the spring. This book provides a resource to facilitate those conversations between young and old, between creation and Creator. These conversations nurture the stuff of life that lies at the heart of every child, every human being—so that every person on Turtle Island will be able to stand on the earth and hear it welcome them back, so that we might understand what it means to be a human being. This book helps to build those relationships with the earth and with each other.

Wisdom is like a river that flows from Creator. Understanding comes when we enter this river that has flown through the land and our ancestors. The task of learning the dances and stories of this land helps us find the wisdom stored up in all of creation. The authors of this book have provided a way forward on the journey through the land that is our life toward the wisdom that will lie at the end.

All my relatives.

*****

Ray Aldred is Cree from Treaty 8 and is also related to the Métis. He is director of the Indigenous Studies Program at the Vancouver School of Theology. He is married to Elaine and has four children, two sons-in-law and two grandchildren. He is a teller of stories he has heard from the many relatives that make up life: the no legged, the four legged, the winged and the two legged.

Foreword by Steve Bell

AS YOU WILL SOON LEARN ABOUT HOW TO RIGHTLY APPROACH AN HONOUR DRUM, I HOPE YOU HAVE ALSO COME TO this book "in a good way." That is, with a humble and grateful receptivity to the precious gift of another's storied wisdom. You, no doubt, have your own story as well and will read this through your unique lens. This is inescapable. But we need not see the world of storied wisdom as an aggressive and competitive zero sum game where there will be inevitable winners and losers. Rather, the wonder of story is that, when it is shared and received in a good way, our own worlds expand and inflate, and new possibilities emerge. Best of all, vital mutuality is forged: enduring friendships marked by grace and beatitude.

The best of children's books—and I believe the one you hold in your hands is among them—contain a hidden depth. They are filled with the enchanting delights of rhyme and colour and shape and discovery. But these are like the tip of the iceberg whose glimmering surface veils the silent mass below. There is a mass of sadness and loss undergirding this "tender little book." However, the tender mutuality of its authors and their loving attention and care to each word and image are themselves a testament to the splendours of redemption (re-creation) that can rise from the depths to catch the blaze of the sun, delight the eyes and fill the heart with hope-filled wonder.

Post the Truth and Reconciliation Commission, this book is a most helpful resource to guide us as we continue down the path toward the healing of relations between Indigenous and settler peoples.

*****

Steve Bell is a singer/songwriter living with his wife, Nanci, in Winnipeg, Manitoba, Treaty 1 Territory and homeland of the Métis Nation. Together they have four adult children, one son-in-law, two daughters-in-law and five grandchildren. Steve's music and advocacy work have been awarded with two Juno Awards and the Queen Elizabeth II Diamond Jubilee Medal. At the time of this book's release, Steve is working on his 20th CD release, *Where the Good Way Lies.*

Dear Parents and Teachers

FROM CHERYL AND TIM

BEFORE YOU ENTER INTO THIS BOOK WITH THE CHILDREN IN YOUR CARE, WE WANT TO SHARE A FEW WORDS ABOUT who we are, how this book came together, how you might use it and how we hope it is received.

We—Cheryl and Tim—come from very different homes, but both abide in the same notion of home. We both celebrate Creator's goodness. We dwell in very distinct regions of an enormous country, but both are in awe of the entire nation's beauty and diversity. In so many lovely ways, we are more alike than different.

However, the history of our lineages surely tells a different story. The sacred bloodline of an Indigenous woman from Canada's west coast and the branches of a Toronto-born Anglo-Canadian man's family tree cross at complex intersections. Canada at-large knows this uneasy kind of reality from east to west, north to south, only too well.

Crafting this children's book together has been more than a shared project—rather, a shared experience. Vital questions, harsh realities and sophisticated conversations do not filter simply into a children's book such as this. But they have been imperative on this journey, just as they are for the entire country of Canada—and they have certainly informed *The Honour Drum*'s purpose and driven its outcome. Grace and humility, truth and reconciliation, transparency and respect, beauty and newness, have all been, and are, at the centre of our tender little book. Better yet, at the centre of our shared story in creating it.

The book has been designed so that you can walk children through it in a variety of ways. We suggest that a first reading might simply have you follow the rhyming stanza and illustration pages in sequence, sparking intrigue and introducing the book's content and themes. After, revisit the book using the accompanying Parent and Teacher Discussion Guide pages to open up meaningful teaching and learning conversation. Depending on the age and interest of the child or children you are sharing this book with, you might work through it over several days, incorporating further research, writing and arts projects. The discussion guide pages have been written so that you will have meaningful content to work with for children of all ages, allowing you to discern age-appropriate language and follow-up.

Ultimately, what follows is not the singular outcome of an Indigenous Canadian woman crafting this very special children's book. Nor is it the implausible outcome of a non-Indigenous Canadian man ridiculously attempting the same. For all of its best intentions and imperfections, it is the humble end result of two dear friends trying to live out and share authentic truth and walk out the journey of reconciliation.

The stanzas are written in our shared voice. The discussion guide is borne from Cheryl's life experience and reasonings and written from Cheryl's perspective, complemented by Tim's input. Tim's illustrations were processed carefully and thoughtfully, always with Cheryl's guidance.

We invite you to receive our shared book as one or more of the following things:

A starting place for learning and insight that are vital and, for so many people of all ages, long overdue. A stark reminder of great truth and beauty that should not, and cannot, be ignored. And of course, a love letter to the Indigenous peoples of Canada, and a humble bow to Indigenous cultures around the globe.

Teach the children in your midst well and learn alongside them. Not simply for the sake of knowledge, but also, no less, for the sake of transformation. And for all the blessings awaiting those with hearts and minds that seek to live in a good way.

Welcome to *The Honour Drum*.

Author's Acknowledgements

GREAT AND HUMBLE THANKS TO RAY ALDRED (CREE) AND STEVE BELL FOR CONTRIBUTING MEANINGFUL AND GENEROUS forewords and for the light they bring in how each uniquely leads his life and speaks into others'.

The west coast First Nations image on the cover of the book is an adaptation of Virgil Dawson's original artwork that appears on Cheryl Bear's personal hand drum. Virgil is from the Kwakwaka'wakw and Sekani Nations in British Columbia. This image is of the thunderbird (middle), raven (left wing), eagle (right wing) and human being at centre. This art also appears in the photo on page 30. Thank you, Virgil, for sharing your beautiful art.

The grey background photos on the stanza-illustration pages of this book are used with permission and were taken and/ or provided by Tommy Alley, Walt Beazley, Cheryl Bear, Nanci Bell, Tim Huff, Michelle Miller, Kevin Clark Studios, Kendara Thompson and Wiconi Living Waters Pow Wow. Among the background images included are: Fancy Shawl dancer Nyla Carpenter (Tahltan and Kaska First Nation); Kiernan Thompson (Oji-Cree); grandfather and grandson Richard Twiss (Sicangu Lakota) and Ezra Twiss (Sicangu Lakota and Diné); Cheryl Bear's cousin Jaden West (Nadleh Whut'en, Bear Clan) and images from the Nadleh Whut'en community. The centre illustration on page 12, regarding Pow Wow, is a representation of Darin Cadman Sr. (men's northern traditional regalia, Kickapoo/Navajo). The wolf mask in the illustration on page 10 is based on a carving by Jason Patrick from Saik'uz, First Nation, in BC, in 2015 and is used by permission.

Truly, we are both so profoundly thankful for our priceless families and the dear friends who faithfully pour goodness into each of our lives. However, with limited space available here, we are unable to name all of the loving and supportive people who have shaped our worlds and mean so much to us. Our sincerest hope as you read this, and certainly when we are with you in person, is that you would know how beloved, valued, appreciated and esteemed you are. Endless thanks, much love!

Referencing supports that have shaped this unique project in a distinct manner and/or share in the vision of where it might lead, we humbly acknowledge and thank: Allison and Tommy Alley, Terri and Miller Alloway and the Maranatha and Lightworks Foundations, Charles Brower (Alaska Inuit), the Compassion Series Council and Youth Unlimited Toronto, Harmony Through Harmony, the Muskoka Woods family, the Signpost Music family, the Nadleh Whut'en First Nations community in British Columbia, Maggie and Greg Paul, Tamara and Bruce Simmonds, all of our dear and inspirational Street Level kin nationwide and the agencies and ministries they represent, The Honourable David C. Onley, Kelly and Brad Pedersen and the Tech4Kids team, Wendy Beauchemin Peterson (Métis), the late Dr. Richard Twiss (Sicangu Lakota) and the NAIITS community (North American Indigenous Institute of Theological Studies), The Honourable Hilary M. Weston, The Word Guild and Youth Unlimited (YFC) chapters across Canada and the national office.

Likewise, as we have both endeavoured in unique full-time community-building, social justice and charitable work and engagement our entire adult lives—across Canada and around the world—we share in our thanksgiving for the countless individuals, families, groups, agencies, schools, businesses and churches that have shown, and continue to show, their support in a myriad of ways.

Of course, we also share in great and many thanks to Larry and Marina Willard and Castle Quay Books for believing in and supporting this special project. And for your graciousness and goodness at every stage.

VERY SPECIAL THANKS AND ACKNOWLEDGEMENT

IT WOULD BE A GREAT INJUSTICE TO NOT SHARE WORDS OF "VERY SPECIAL THANKS" TO, AND GREAT ACKNOWLEDGEMENT of, Julia Beazley. Julia's work and care for this project have been profound. Julia has committed her life and voice to championing wellness and meaningful change around complex and vital matters of social justice in Canada. Her combined talent and heart are incredible. Julia's personal and professional engagement on this project have been priceless. Best of all, we both love her like a sister.

the HONOUR drum

Look to the people of age and of youth
With a history of wisdom, of honour and truth.

They come to the drum, it's the heartbeat of earth
They know of its value, assured of its worth.

Theirs is the music of story and chant
Songs from the heart, songs of the dance.

Dances of meaning, movements of life
Of wonder and family, free from all strife.

Patterns and symbols and colours abound
Like the blues of the sky and the greens of the ground.

Pow Wow is a time to gather and meet
To sing and remember, to dance and to eat.

Totem poles too have a story to tell
Of nations and chiefs and families that dwell.

Important are stories to hear and to tell
History, values and humour as well.

Elders are keepers of stories and tales;
Respected and honoured, their wisdom prevails.

The words we use matter, to help understand
Like the word "Indigenous"; it means "of the land."

Indigenous people, each in their own way
Have a name for Creator, to speak and to pray.

We honour Creator by caring well for
All of creation—shore to shore to shore.

Imagine if there were an honour drum
Where all children gathered, wherever they're from.

To listen, respect, to learn and to share
For this is the way to show that you care.

Look to the people of age and of youth
With a history of wisdom, of honour and truth.

INDIGENOUS PEOPLES HAVE BEEN IN NORTH AMERICA SINCE TIME IMMEMORIAL, MEANING FOR AS LONG AS CAN BE remembered. Much has changed over the centuries, such as housing. This illustration depicts the kinds of dwellings some of the peoples would have lived in: a longhouse or "big house" from the Pacific Northwest, a Plains tipi (teepee), an igloo from the north, and a longhouse from Eastern Canada. Indigenous people do not live in these types of housing anymore, but they are still used for ceremony, display or teaching.

Typically, the history of Canada starts with the immigrant story.

However, this is a one-sided story that has been told many times. The Indigenous story is quite a different story. Our story starts with Creator.

In our oral traditions, or our oral history, the elders teach that Creator placed us on our land.

There were many different Indigenous peoples here on Turtle Island (which is what some Indigenous people call North America). There were and still are hundreds of different Indigenous languages, customs and traditions.

The history of Indigenous peoples since the arrival of the European settlers is a complex one, and in many ways we are all still trying to learn to walk together in a good way, as neighbours. Listening and learning with humility and understanding are vital to finding that way forward.

Here in Canada, we are always trying to find ways to relate to each other and talk about our sameness, and that is right and good. But it's also important to celebrate and value the ways we are vastly different. Indigenous worldview (way of being), values (the beliefs that shape what we do and how we do it) and cultures (everything from art, music, food, clothing and how we hunt) are quite different, not only among Indigenous people but also from that of the mainstream North American culture.

DISCUSSION QUESTIONS

1. Have you ever heard the story of Canada from an Indigenous perspective?

2. Which Indigenous community is closest to where you live? (If you do not know, we suggest that it is important to look this up with your class or family.) Do you have any Indigenous friends?

3. Do you know which Indigenous community's traditional land you are on? The Indigenous community closest to you likely has a treaty with Canada. Do you know what it means to live in a treaty relationship with that Indigenous community? Taking some time to research and find out the answers is very meaningful. This is very important to know, because understanding this is part of what it means to be a Canadian.

They come to the drum,
it's the heartbeat of earth
They know of its value,
assured of its worth.

THIS ILLUSTRATION INCLUDES A POW WOW DRUM, AN INUIT HAND DRUM, A TRADITIONAL MÉTIS HAND DRUM AND Cheryl Bear with her First Nations hand drum.

There is a common belief among Indigenous peoples that the drumbeat is the "heartbeat of Mother Earth." It is considered sacred, and you are only to sit at the drum if you are living in a "good and honourable way."

The drum may come in different shapes and sizes, and distinct types are used by different communities. Some communities use a hand drum. Others have a floor drum, also called a big drum or Pow Wow drum (like the one in the cover illustration).

The drum rims are made of wood. Cedar, in particular, is strong and has a lovely smell. The skin of the drum is made of different animal hides, like deer, elk, moose or buffalo. The sinew of the animal (which is like the gristle on a steak that you can't chew through) is used as string to hold the drum together. Some Inuit drums are made with the intestines of whales or walruses. The process of making a drum is detailed and precise.

Those who sit at the drum must come to it "in a good way." This is a common phrase among Indigenous people. "In a good way" means they start with prayer and make their hearts right before Creator. The elders tell us that when you hit the drum, whatever is in your heart will come out and affect the people who listen. If there is anger or sadness in your heart, the people will feel it. So you have to be cleansed before you come to the drum, so the people feel good and happy as they listen.

When you hear an Indigenous drum it evokes unique emotions. It's different from when you hear a marching drum or a drum kit; it is like a call, and you feel it deep in your soul. The sound of the drum brings everyone together.

Caring for your drum is important. When you have a drum, you are to treat it with the utmost respect. If the drum is too warm, you should put it in a cool place. If it is cold, you should wrap it in a blanket. When it is not being used, it should be kept covered. Covering is an indication of its worth and value.

Note for teachers and parents: We suggest you find a video online of a Pow Wow drum group.

DISCUSSION QUESTIONS

1. Are there drums or percussion instruments in your family tradition?

2. If so, what do they look and sound like?

3. Do you know the story of the drums in your tradition or culture?

4. How do you feel when you hear a drumbeat?

Theirs is the music of story and chant
Songs from the heart, songs of the dance.

IN THIS PICTURE, YOU SEE A MÉTIS FIDDLE, INUIT THROAT SINGERS AND A TURTLE RATTLE.

Every Indigenous community has its own unique musical traditions, including songs, instruments and dances. Instruments vary from drums to guitars to fiddles. Drums and rattles are percussion instruments that are traditionally used by First Nations people. The instruments, songs and dance all work together and are an important expression of family, community and story.

There are different styles of traditional singing—some with words and some with vocal sounds and chants. Chants are called vocables. An elder once said the chant represents the deepest cry of one's heart. Some Pow Wow songs belong to certain individuals and can be used to tell a personal story. There are victory songs, flag songs and two-step songs for a couple's dance during a Pow Wow.

To some people, the chants and Pow Wow songs can all sound quite similar. But for Indigenous people, each song is recognized as unique in style and meaning.

Inuit throat singing is a unique kind of chant. The performers are usually women or girls, and they sing in duets in a kind of contest to see who can outlast the other and sometimes who can go longest without giggling.

For many years after Europeans came to North America, Indigenous people were not allowed to practice their ceremonies (like the west coast Potlatch and the Plains Sun Dance), music or songs. Remembering, teaching and sharing those traditions, as well as Indigenous languages, are all important ways of honouring Indigenous people and preserving our cultures.

Note for teachers and parents: You can look for examples of Inuit throat singers online.

DISCUSSION QUESTIONS

1. Does your family tradition have a special style of music that represents you?

2. If so, what kinds of instruments are involved?

3. Do you play any of those instruments?

4. What other instruments interest you, and why?

Dances of meaning,
movements of life

Of wonder and family,
free from all strife.

THIS PICTURE SHOWS THREE INDIGENOUS DANCERS FROM DIFFERENT PARTS OF CANADA. THERE IS A MÉTIS JIGGER, A west coast dancer in traditional regalia and a Gwich'in dancer from the Northwest Territories.

Every Indigenous community has its own style of dancing, and it is a very important and unique part of the culture. Dancing is not only fun and social but also a spiritual act, and every step of the dance is a prayer.

On the west coast, they dance in family groups. For example, when someone starts singing the Bear Clan song, everyone in the Bear Clan honours the song by dancing. It's a way of celebrating the family and each other, and it makes everybody happy.

Many Inuit "motion" dances belong to a person, family or dance group and tell of personal experiences. These songs and dances may be "gifted" to other groups to learn and dance.

There are some stereotypes about Indigenous dance—for example, that all Indigenous people do the Rain Dance. While there are peoples who perform Rain Dances, different groups have a variety of dances with various purposes. Some dances are ceremonial, like the Sun Dance of the Plains peoples. There are traditional men's dances and traditional women's dances. The Red River Jig is a traditional dance of the Métis.

The Jingle Dress Dance, for example, is a healing dance. The dance was given in a dream to a man whose daughter was sick, after he prayed to Creator for help. The father was shown the dance and how to make the jingle dress. The girl put on the dress and danced as she was told, and as she danced she became stronger and got better. Today, the dance is performed in honour of community members who are sick or need healing.

DISCUSSION QUESTIONS

1. Lots of cultures have their own unique dances. How many dances from around the world can you think of (for example, Hula, Highland dancing, Maori Haka, Irish step dancing)?

2. Are there dances in your family tradition?

3. If so, can you explain what the dances mean or where they come from? If not, it is fun and meaningful to find out.

Patterns and symbols and colours abound
Like the blues of the sky and the greens of the ground.

IN THIS PICTURE ARE SOME EXAMPLES OF INDIGENOUS CLOTHING AND CEREMONIAL ITEMS, INCLUDING A HAT, mukluks, a headdress, a blanket and a mask. Indigenous people refer to our traditional clothing as regalia, which means special dress or ceremonial clothes. Every Indigenous group has its own distinctive style of dress, and you can often tell where someone is from by looking at their clothes, their hats or headdresses, or the ornamentation they wear.

The colours and designs, stitching, beadwork and weaving are unique, intricate and beautiful and have great meaning to the people they belong to. Masks are distinctive of the west coast peoples, and each people group has a particular style of art and carving.

Only certain leaders from a small number of Indigenous communities are allowed to wear the headdress. They are generally worn by males of the Plains Indigenous communities who hold a place of honour in the community, like a chief. Whoever is wearing a headdress is a significant person in the community.

Mukluks are traditional to the Dene people of the north. Inuit mukluks, or qamiq, are sewn from caribou or wolf skins. The soles may be made of sealskin or caribou hide, with the hair on the inside for warmth. The fancy trim (kuupaqs) on the mukluks might be sewn from other skins in intricate and individual designs. Glass beads were a later addition to Indigenous clothing and regalia, brought to North America by settler peoples and used in trade. Prior to this, natural materials like shells, quills, seeds and bones were used to create the designs.

It is important to address the injustice of cultural appropriation, which is the use of elements, symbols or traditional dress of one culture by members of another. Some people dress up as Indigenous people for Halloween or costume parties. Fashion designers incorporate Indigenous styles on their runways, and pop stars sometimes use our regalia to be trendy.

This is deeply troubling to Indigenous people. For example, if a headdress is inappropriate even for some Indigenous people to wear, it is highly inappropriate for anyone else. The headdress is significant to discuss here because it is not something that an Indigenous person would ever just go and buy. It has to come to you in a good way. It is a very prestigious honour. If the giving of one eagle feather is the highest honour one can give another person, an entire headdress with eagle feathers is very significant. A non-Indigenous person wearing a headdress is comparable to a non-military person wearing a military uniform and stars of a general.

For things to change, our terminology and our way of thinking about Indigenous regalia must change. We can no longer refer to Indigenous cultural clothing as a "costume." A costume is something you wear when you are pretending to be something else. When Indigenous people wear traditional clothing, we are being our true selves.

DISCUSSION QUESTIONS

1. Does your family or culture have any symbols or patterns that are meaningful or sacred (for example, family crest, tartan, coat of arms)?

2. If so, what do they represent?

3. What Indigenous regalia are you most familiar with? Where have you seen it?

Pow Wow is a time to gather and meet
To sing and remember, to dance and to eat.

THIS ILLUSTRATION IS OF THREE FIRST NATIONS MEN IN A GRAND ENTRY AT A POW WOW. A POW WOW IS A SOCIAL gathering held by many different Indigenous communities across Canada and the USA. It is a time for the communities to gather, sing, dance, socialize and honour and celebrate their cultures. Everyone is welcome at the Pow Wow. There is often a dance competition, with dancers wearing beautiful and intricate regalia. Often there are many drum groups that sing in rotation. It is fun and challenging for the drum groups because they don't know what kind of song they'll be asked to sing. Therefore the drum teams must memorize many songs and be ready immediately when they are called on. Sometimes a dancer may request a special song from a favourite drum team. The dancer asks in a good way with a ceremonial gift. A ceremonial gift or money is dropped on the drum if a drum team is singing a favourite song particularly well. This is always an honour and also great fun because the whole Pow Wow community gathers around the drum to dance and sing the song.

Not all Indigenous peoples have Pow Wows. West coast peoples, for example, have the Potlatch, which is a political, economic and social gathering. People sit with their clans and do business.

Food is a central part of any First Nations celebration or gathering. A favourite food of Indigenous peoples of Canada is a fried bread or baked bread called bannock, which, though it was brought over by the Europeans, has become a favourite traditional food.

Gathering and preparing foods are also important parts of our culture. On the west coast, August and September are spent harvesting salmon, cleaning and preparing it for canning, drying and smoking. Most families have a smokehouse, where the meat is prepared. Once it is dried and smoked, it becomes like a jerky. Some meats, like moose, can be dried and canned. One moose can feed a family for about a year. Deer and elk are also traditional foods.

The Inuit traditionally hunted oil- and fat-rich foods like whale and seal.

Berry picking is an important part of many communities. There are specific times to pick huckleberries and saskatoon berries. On the west coast, some communities pick soap berries, or Nwus (Dakelh language), with great anticipation because they are whipped into what is still called Indian Ice Cream, an all-time favourite.

DISCUSSION QUESTIONS

1. What kind of "all are welcome" celebrations have you been to?

2. Does your family or culture have any foods that are traditional?

3. Are there special ways that the foods are prepared?

4. Have you tried foods from other cultures? Did you find them very different from your own?

Totem poles too
have a story to tell
Of nations and chiefs
and families that dwell.

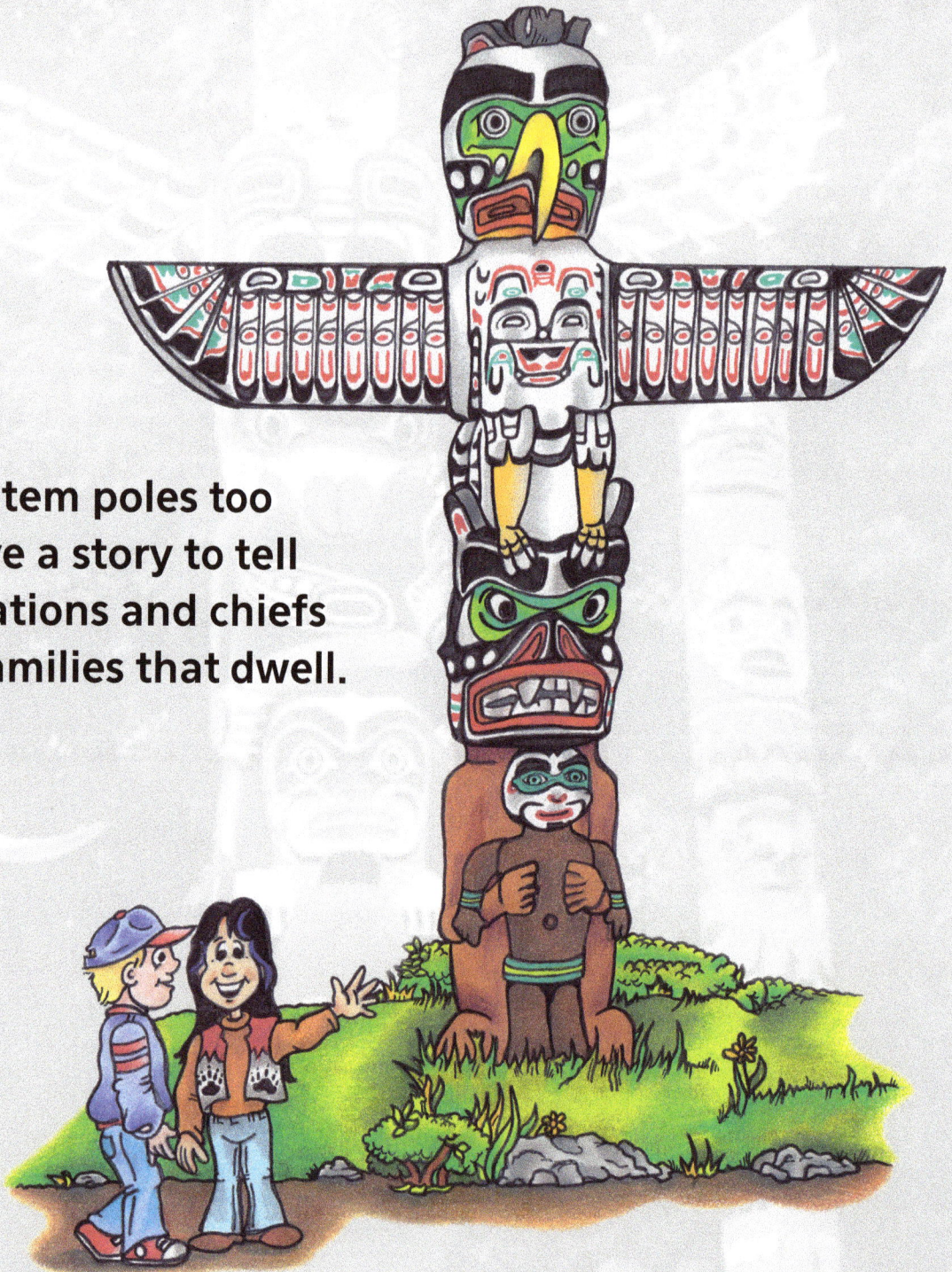

IT IS OFTEN ASSUMED THAT ALL INDIGENOUS PEOPLE IN CANADA AND THE USA HAVE TOTEM POLES AND LIVE—OR lived—in tipis. But this is a stereotype. In this picture, we see a totem pole. A totem pole is a large sculpture carved on a pole or large tree, yellow or red cedar, by Indigenous peoples of the Pacific Northwest. It is one of the most recognizable cultural symbols of the Pacific Northwest, and even other countries of the world know about totem poles. This particular totem pole is based on one from Stanley Park in Vancouver, BC. (The background photo also represents the well-known totem poles in Stanley Park.) Authentic totem poles are found only on the west coast, in Washington State, British Columbia and Alaska.

While totem poles are sometimes found elsewhere, even with the best of intentions the use of an inauthentic totem pole is disrespectful to west coast Indigenous people. Any replications should be used with permission and used to honour a people, not misrepresent them further.

The images on the totem are usually of beings, or animals, which represent different clans, and every clan is a family group. The figures on the totem pole mark a family's lineage. I (Cheryl Bear) am of the Bear Clan, so when I see a bear on a totem pole, it makes me feel proud and connected.

The tree used for the totem is chosen carefully for its beauty, character and uniqueness. Before the tree is cut down, it is honoured and shown great respect.

Some people assume that totem poles are religious symbols, but they are not. Totem poles are a way of recording the story of a chief or family and sometimes even point the way to a good fishing spot.

Ancient cultures used oral tradition to tell their story. By story, we don't mean legend, myth or fable; we mean our history, the story of our people. The totem pole is a means of communicating our history. It is a way of telling the histories or ancestry of a family, a clan or a community. This means the stories were passed down through generations through the telling of the story, with song, stone, oratory or carving, rather than by writing it down.

Some non-Indigenous people may find totems and Indigenous artwork alarming, but it is just a different style of art that may be unfamiliar. I (Cheryl Bear) have often found abstract art to be daunting, or even scary, but once I took the time to understand what it represented, I gained a different appreciation for it.

DISCUSSION QUESTIONS

1. What are some of the clans you see represented on the totem pole in the picture?

2. Have you ever seen a totem pole? If so, where?

3. Does your family have any kind of symbol (for example, crest, tartan)?

Important are stories to hear and to tell
History, values and humour as well.

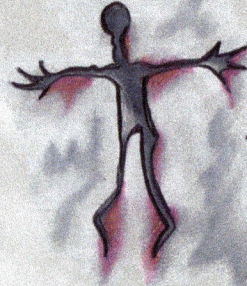

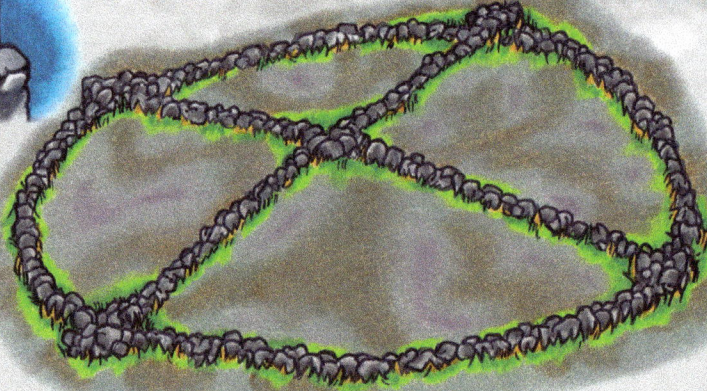

THIS IS A PICTURE OF AN INUIT INUKSUK (INUKSHUK), A MEDICINE WHEEL AND SOME ANCIENT STONE ETCHINGS.

All of these tell stories and communicate the truths of a people. Stories and language contain our identity. We are tied to generations past through our stories.

Oral tradition is a way to remember your history. This is common all over the world in Indigenous cultures and is even the way we remembered ancient stories, like the teachings of great thinkers, philosophers and religious leaders, before they were in written form.

Indigenous people have very intricate political systems. When the Europeans arrived in North America, they believed their ways were superior to those of the Indigenous people. They soon became the dominant culture, partly because of the decimation of Indigenous populations due to diseases brought from Europe.

In the dominant culture, spoken stories became irrelevant because the written word was considered more accurate. But oral and non-written traditions are powerful means of communicating truth. Stories have the ability to transform us and to help us live better lives. Indigenous people have always known the power of story.

Some of our stories are history, some are warnings, and some are just plain fun. Some stories involve a character called the trickster. On the west coast, the trickster is the raven. In the Plains, it is the coyote. The trickster is a valuable part of the community. The trickster represents conflict. Whenever we are faced with conflict, it is an opportunity for growth and change, and that is what these stories represent. They are told in a metaphorical way, so you listen, think about them for a long time, and then apply the truths to your own life.

DISCUSSION QUESTIONS

1. Often there are stories within families that are passed down from generation to generation. They might be funny stories about a relative or a close family friend. Are there any stories like that in your family?

2. In your community or culture, are there stories that are told and retold?

3. Can you tell us a story—the history of your family, a funny story about a relative or a story with a moral?

Elders are keepers of stories and tales;
Respected and honoured, their wisdom prevails.

THIS IS A PICTURE OF AN INDIGENOUS ELDER AND SOME YOUNG PEOPLE GATHERED AROUND TO LISTEN AND LEARN.

Indigenous people never use the term "senior citizen." We use the word "elder," because it is a term of deep respect and honour. The symbol for wisdom in Indigenous culture is a circle of elders.

Indigenous communities generally seek the wisdom and advice of our elders. They have secrets to tell us that can help us live good and happy lives. When an elder speaks, you have to listen. One of the ways we show respect to our elders is to listen until they are finished speaking, without interrupting.

Elders are the storykeepers of our communities, which makes their role very important. The story is the foundation of our history and identity as Indigenous people.

There is a beautiful dynamic called community memory that emerges when you're among a group of elders, telling the stories of a people. When we are together, we remember more. We remember stories, jokes and lessons. We share ideas, and everyone participates. We are stronger when we are together. The emphasis in Indigenous culture is not on the individual but on everyone together. Elders are the ones who carry the community. They help ease the competitiveness in a community in discussions around political and social issues. They level the playing field and help everyone work together.

In Indigenous culture, grandparents play a significant role in raising children. In times past, grandparents, parents and children would all live together in the same house. The parents were responsible for everyone's food and shelter, while the grandparents' role was to teach the children Indigenous values, way of being and how to behave. They would also teach children skills like cleaning fish and gathering and preparing food.

Grandparents are storytellers, which is important to maintaining the oral tradition of a community.

DISCUSSION QUESTIONS

1. Who are the elders in your life?

2. What role do your elders play in your family or community?

3. Have you asked your grandparents or the elders in your life what life was like when they were your age? How was it different from yours?

The words we use matter, to help understand
Like the word "Indigenous"; it means "of the land."

IN THIS PICTURE, YOU SEE AN EAGLE FEATHER, AN INUKSUK (INUKSHUK) AND A MÉTIS SASH. THESE ARE ALL IMPORTANT symbols for Canada's first or Indigenous peoples. Our Indigenous peoples include First Nations, Inuit and Métis.

You may have heard all kinds of names, like Indians, Native, Eskimo, Aboriginal or First Nations. Indigenous people in Canada were formerly referred to as Indians. This is because when Columbus landed in North America, he was actually looking for India. The term "Indian" was then officially replaced by "Aboriginal," which means "of unknown origin," which isn't quite right either. The preferred term is "Indigenous," which actually means "of the land." The word "Indigenous" incorporates First Nations, Métis and Inuit, which are three distinct people groups in Canada.

But the best term to use indicates where one is from. For example, I (Cheryl Bear) am Nadleh Whut'en from the Dakelh Nation. This is the best and most honouring way to introduce me. Because this is my place, where I am from, I only introduce myself in this way. When you refer to an Indigenous person, it is most honouring to say his or her community and people group.

The eagle feather is the most sacred and honoured gift you can give or receive in Indigenous culture. It is important to know the story of the feather—where it came from, how it was found and how it came to you. If it's given to you, it's a high honour. If you find it, it's a gift from the eagle and a sign from Creator.

The Inuksuk is a human-made stone landmark found from Alaska to Greenland. The word "Inuksuk" means "something that acts for or performs the function of a person." Traditionally, it was used to point the way, to mark an important or meaningful site or as a marker to say someone was here. Inuksuk is an important Inuit cultural symbol.

The Métis sash is a finger-woven belt made of brightly coloured wool. It had all kinds of uses traditionally, but the Métis men wore it around the waist and used it to carry belongings during the fur trade. The colours in the sash are meaningful and identify allegiances and honours or have historical significance. The sashes had all kinds of uses, but they are most well known for being worn by the voyageurs as they paddled their canoes. Today, the sash is worn by members of the Métis nation as a symbol of nationhood and pride. Men wear it around their waist, while women wear it draped over one shoulder and loosely tied at waist level.

DISCUSSION QUESTIONS

1. Canada has been enriched by Indigenous values, culture and knowledge. For example, the harvesting of maple syrup was indigenous to eastern peoples and given to settlers. Also, the canoe was invented by Indigenous peoples and adopted by fur traders. Can you think of other examples?

2. It can be very hurtful to be called an inappropriate name or racial slur. This is unkind and a form of bullying. How do we approach all of the different cultures and religions in Canada respectfully? (Parents and teachers, here is where you can contextualize the conversation for your own family or class and the cultures and faiths represented in your community.)

Indigenous people, each in their own way
Have a name for Creator, to speak and to pray.

THERE IS A NAME FOR CREATOR IN EVERY FIRST NATIONS COMMUNITY IN CANADA AND THE UNITED STATES. EVERY Pow Wow, Potlatch, ceremony and meeting (whether social, tribal meeting or business) is opened with prayer to Creator. Indigenous people are very spiritual people who believe the land and animals need to be cared for and are sacred.

This concept of Creator is ancient and predates contact with Europeans. Creator is the one who made everything, hears our prayers, watches over us, guides us, provides for us, deserves our gratitude and respect, sees all, knows all and loves all. Some of the names of Creator in English are the Great Spirit, the Great Mystery, the Being Up on High and the One Who Started Everything.

Most Indigenous cultures believe their name for Creator deserves too much respect to be written down or shared in any way other than orally. There is a story of a Navajo elder who refused to give the name of Creator in Dene to an anthropologist. He would only give the English translation because even the name of Creator deserved so much respect.

The foundation of many ceremonies is the belief in Creator, who is approached with prayer, fasting, ceremony and cleansing. A well-known ceremony for young men is called a vision quest. It is a coming-of-age ceremony where the young man goes into the forest for a time of fasting and prayer to receive a vision from Creator. There is also a significant coming-of-age ceremony for a young woman that is a celebration of her reaching maturity.

There is a beautiful cleansing ceremony called the smudge. Sage (or cedar or sweetgrass) is lit, and then the fire is extinguished. A scented smoke will rise from the dried sage and is placed in a bowl (typically abalone shell). The person leading the ceremony will push the smoke towards someone with an eagle feather, and that person will pull the smoke toward themselves and ceremonially apply the smoke to themselves. It is a beautiful ceremony where we deal with emotional wounds, ceremonially washing these things away from ourselves.

DISCUSSION QUESTIONS

1. Does your culture or religion have any ceremonies or traditions to mark a rite of passage or coming of age (for example, bar mitzvah or bat mitzvah, confirmation, baptism, quinceanera)?

2. What good and inspiring words have you heard used to describe Creator, God or a deity in your family or culture?

SPECIAL NOTE: The background photo on page 22 is from the Nadleh Whut'en First Nation in British Columbia, Canada. "Nadleh" means "The Place Where the Salmon Return." The Indigenous people from this area are called Dakelh, which means "The People Who Travel the Water."

We honour Creator by caring well for
All of creation—shore to shore to shore.

"MOTHER EARTH" IS A TERM THAT DENOTES OUR DEPENDENCE ON THE EARTH FOR OUR SURVIVAL. SHE IS DEFINITELY like a mother who gives us water to drink and food to eat but also can show her strength (in the wind, rain and snow) and deserves great respect. The earth is sacred. Creator is called upon to provide and care for us, and the earth is a great gift that we must respect and be grateful for.

When Indigenous people meet, we don't ask what each other does; we ask where each other is from. This is because Indigenous people identify with place first. What you do is not as important as where you are from. Indigenous peoples are very connected to land and to place, and land is connected to identity. Who we are is connected to not only a people but also a sacred place.

In our stories, Creator placed us on our traditional lands. Creator gave us land not to own but to watch over and to care well for, and this makes our land a sacred place. Creator gave us this land to share with others. The idea of owning land is not a traditional understanding among Indigenous people. As one of the great chiefs said, "You cannot own the land any more than you can own the air." First Nations value that it is our responsibility to watch over, care for and respect the earth and all living creatures. Creator is made known and revealed through creation.

Often in the news, there are stories of social issues and inadequate infrastructure in some Indigenous communities, and non-Indigenous people will commonly ask, "Why don't they just move to the city?" It is because we are tied to the land. It is part of our identity. We love our land. Indigenous people work very hard to preserve and protect our traditional land. Most Indigenous people will be buried in the graveyard on their land, no matter how far away they have travelled.

There is respect for everything that lives and has breath and a belief that everything is connected. Water, land, animals and humans need one another's care to thrive. For Indigenous peoples, hunting is not a sport; it is an act of mutuality. The hunter respects the animal and thanks the animal who gives its life so that we can live. The principle is to only take what you need and to use what you take. So when we hunt, we only take what we need, and we use all parts of the animal for clothing, food, sewing, grease, blankets and shelter.

DISCUSSION QUESTIONS

1. Where does your food come from?

2. How often do we take food for granted and waste food and water? What ways does your family share or conserve food?

3. How often do you get out into nature? What is your favourite place in the outdoors to explore?

Imagine if there were an honour drum
Where all children gathered, wherever they're from.

HERE IN NORTH AMERICA, WE ARE ALWAYS TRYING TO FIND COMMON GROUND. WE LONG FOR WAYS WE CAN CONNECT with one another and instantly find our mutuality. While well-intended, this is not always very honouring. We are looking for sameness, for familiarity, so we can feel comfortable. But sometimes it's good and important to step outside of our comfort zones. We have vast differences that should be acknowledged and even celebrated.

One of the greatest challenges that Indigenous peoples have had to face—and continue to face—is stereotyping. In modern history, movies, television and novels have often perpetuated images and portrayals of North American Indigenous peoples that have been inaccurate, unfair and often unkind.

What had often, and wrongly, been considered harmless fun by many non-Indigenous North Americans is now being recognized for what it is: disrespectful and hurtful. As important as it is to be rid of these stereotypes, it is just as important to replace them with truth.

As discussed earlier, for the Indigenous peoples of Canada, central to the invitation to come to the drum is that one's mind, heart and actions align so that you come "in a good way."

The virtue of goodness is too often overlooked. Maybe it is considered too plain, too subjective or too hard to measure. But it's a shame that goodness—whether given, received or shared—is not given a more central place in the lives of all children, all around the world. Likewise, the Indigenous value of living "in a good way" is a powerful notion for all children and adults.

An important part of goodness is compassion. The word "compassion" is often misunderstood. People often align it with pity or simply feeling sad or sorry for others. Compassion is actually an ancient Latin word. "Com" means "together," and "passion" means "to suffer or endure." So, to be compassionate does not mean to simply feel something but to feel something and come alongside others because of it. Compassion-driven actions, words and mindsets are vital for all people in every part of the world, at all times.

DISCUSSION QUESTIONS

1. This picture shows a diverse group of children gathered together. Many more could be added. If you were to add some children, what might they look like? (Perhaps invite your children/child to draw, or draw with them.)

2. There might be a number of ways the children gathered at this drum are different from you. For example: their language, favourite foods, the activities they enjoy and so on. Can you think of ways that children all over the world are likely similar? (The response you might hope for and encourage would imply "goodness" in the forms of creativity, laughter, friendship, kindness, imagination, etc.)

3. What do you think compassion means? Can you think of an example of someone behaving with compassion?

To listen, respect,
to learn and to share
For this is the way
to show that you care.

LISTENING IS A VALUE OF INDIGENOUS PEOPLES. IT IS A WAY OF HONOURING ONE ANOTHER. IF YOU SPEAK WITH elders, chances are they will be silent for a time after you speak—what will seem like an eternity to many people who dislike "awkward silences." There is no such thing in our culture. Silence is powerful, and it is a way to show respect.

When you are speaking with elders, they will wait for you to finish talking and then will be silent for a time before responding. This pause is a sign of thoughtful and active listening and of wisdom, assuring their most careful response, thinking about every word. Words are never wasted.

This is quite powerful. To listen and pause is to honour someone's thoughts and words. Most of us are far more used to a style of conversation that involves interrupting, interjecting and thinking more about what we will say next than truly hearing what the other person is saying.

Inside the University of British Columbia House of Learning, there are three totem poles, one with its mouth wide open and enlarged, while the other two totems have very large ears. This is to show us we are to listen twice as much as we speak. Listening is honouring. Listening shows humility.

The history of Indigenous peoples of Canada is filled with great beauty, mystery, survival and wonder. However, recent history (the past six centuries) has been much more complex—perhaps best described as devastating and unthinkable. As important as it is to teach all children living in Canada about the beauty of our Indigenous peoples, it is equally important that all Canadians explore the hard truths borne out of the "Doctrine of Discovery" and the grief-filled journey to hopeful newness of "Truth and Reconciliation."

For you—as teacher, parent or caregiver—these might be starting points for your own research and understanding as you seek to teach the children in your care in a manner that is age-appropriate and thoughtful.

DISCUSSION QUESTIONS

1. What have you learned in this book that surprised you? Why?

2. What other questions do you have about the Indigenous peoples of Canada? (This is an opportunity for you to research and learn together.)

3. Has this book helped you better understand Indigenous peoples? If so, how?

Imagine if there were an honour drum...

Cheryl Bear

"**THIS BOOK CELEBRATES THE BEAUTY OF OUR INDIGENOUS PEOPLE IN CANADA AND THE** United States. Yet, we have not told the entire story. The weight of our community story is crushing. An elder once told me, 'We grieve in two ways: we cry and we laugh.' There is so much more I long to tell you: that our people are so very witty and could make you laugh for hours; that our people go from grief to grief because our families are huge and we are connected to hundreds and hundreds of cousins (not even exaggerating). There is such beauty and complexity in our story. I'm grateful you have decided to journey alongside us in this colossal effort of Indigenous and Ally."

Cheryl Bear's First Nation community is Nadleh Whut'en First Nation in British Columbia, Canada. She is from the Dakelh Nation and Dumdenyoo Clan (Bear Clan). She has three young adult sons, Paul, Randall and Justice Barnetson.

Cheryl is well known as an important and respected voice on behalf of Canada's Indigenous peoples, a highly revered speaker and teacher who has travelled to over 600 Indigenous communities in Canada and the United States sharing her songs and stories. She also visits non-Indigenous communities (schools, governments, churches and businesses), holding workshops to raise awareness and understanding of Indigenous issues. But more than anything else, Cheryl's heart is best known in the quietness of time spent with her people.

Cheryl is also a multi-award-winning singer/songwriter who shares stories of Indigenous life: the joy, sorrow, faith and journey, through story and song. She has released three albums: *Cheryl Bear* (self titled), *The Good Road*, and *A' BA*. Cheryl's highly-acclaimed albums have received three Indigenous People's Choice music awards, two Covenant Awards and a Native American Music Award.

She is one of the founding board members of the North American Indigenous Institute of Theological Studies (NAIITS). She is also an associate professor at Regent College, in Vancouver, BC.

Cheryl has an earned doctorate from The King's University in Van Nuys, California, and a master of divinity degree from Regent College, Vancouver, BC, and a bachelor of arts from Pacific Life Bible College in Surrey, BC.

Cheryl was first elected as a band councillor for her community of Nadleh Whut'en First Nation in April 2014 and was re-elected in April 2016.

Cheryl can be reached at: cheryl@cherylbear.com. (Please note, all communications are monitored, and replies are subject to Cheryl's availability and discretion.)

Cheryl's music is available on iTunes.

Tim Huff

"PROFOUNDLY HUMBLED, GREATLY BLESSED AND ENDLESSLY SCHOOLED" ARE THE words Tim uses to synthesize his experiences working alongside Cheryl Bear to craft *The Honour Drum*.

Born and raised in Toronto, Canada, Tim Huff has stitched together a unique life of service among children, youth and adults facing profound physical, intellectual, emotional, social and spiritual challenges. His journey of full-time service, learning and advocacy has taken him across Canada and the United States and around the world, as an avid learner and highly sought-after speaker and teacher regarding proactive community building and compassionate responses to domestic poverty, marginalization and poverty of spirit.

Tim's impressive resumé of direct service and leadership includes: staff director of the Ontario Camp of the Deaf, founding director of Frontlines Youth Centre, founding director of the YU's Light Patrol street outreach, co-founder of The Hope Exchange Street Level Network, member of the boards of directors for The Daily Bread Food Bank and Hockey Helps the Homeless, and chairperson for several national social-justice conferences and campaigns. Tim currently serves as the "Creative and Development Lead" of Youth Unlimited's interactive Compassion Series.

Tim is the author of three award-winning best-sellers for adults: *Bent Hope: A Street Journal*, *Dancing with Dynamite: Celebrating Against the Odds* and *The Yuletide Factor: Cause for Perpetual Comfort and Joy*. He is also the author/illustrator of the award-winning best-selling children's books *The Cardboard Shack Beneath the Bridge: Helping Children Understand Homelessness* and *It's Hard Not to Stare: Helping Children Understand Disabilities*. Tim's writing is also featured in the "O Canada" edition of *Chicken Soup for the Soul*.

In addition to Tim's multiple writing awards, including the prestigious Grace Irwin Award, Tim is the recipient of a number of service awards, including the Queen Elizabeth II Diamond Jubilee Medal.

Tim, married to Diane, is the father of two beloved young adult children: Sarah Jane and Jake. Tim also fronts the band Outrider—covering classic rock songs that speak about hope, life and celebration.

For more information on Tim's books for adults and children, information on booking Tim to speak, the link to Tim's TEDx Talk ("The Only To-Do List that Matters") and information about Youth Unlimited's Compassion Series program and resources go to **www.compassionseries.com**.

Tim's books are available through most retail distributors in Canada and the USA, including Indigo, Chapters, Barnes and Noble and Baker and Taylor, and in 27 other countries around the world, including the United Kingdom and Australia. Also available in e-book format through Amazon (Kindle) and Apple (iTunes). Best pricing and quick delivery are available at **www.castlequaybooks.com**.

CASTLE QUAY BOOKS
WWW.CASTLEQUAYBOOKS.COM

COMPASSION SERIES BOOKS FOR CHILDREN BY TIM HUFF AND FRIENDS

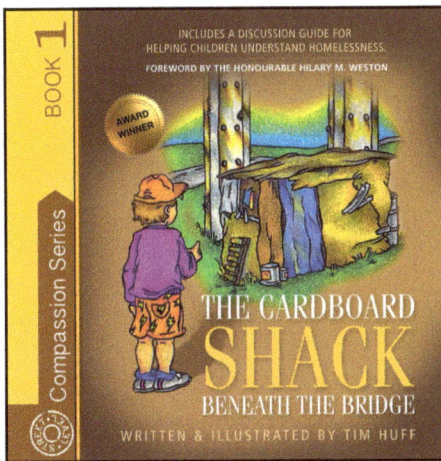

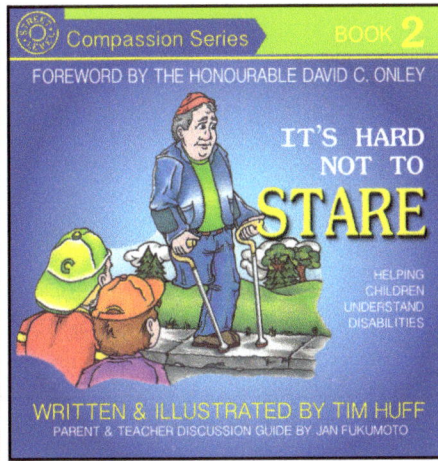

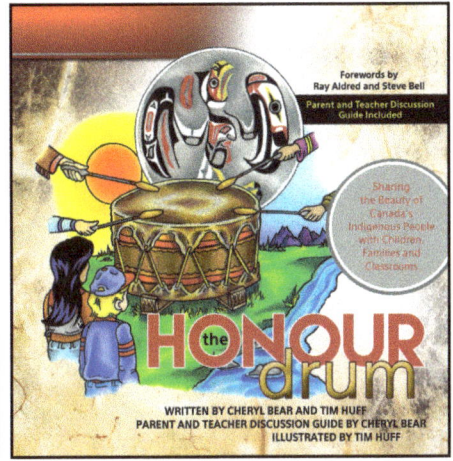

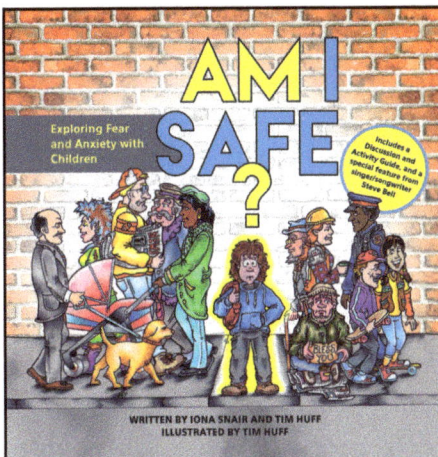

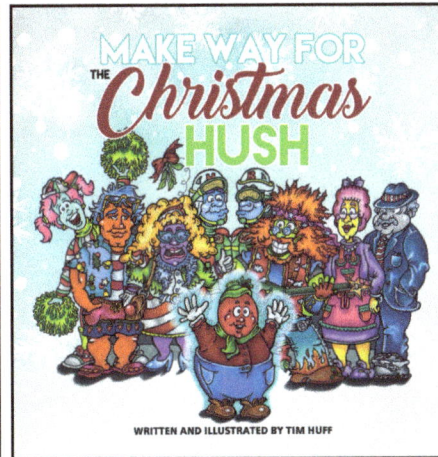

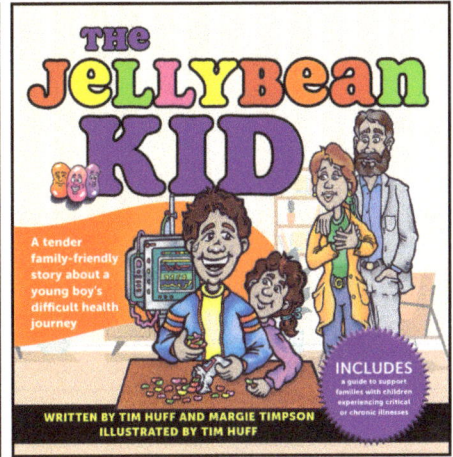

BOOK 1

Compassion Series

INCLUDES A DISCUSSION GUIDE FOR HELPING CHILDREN UNDERSTAND HOMELESSNESS.

FOREWORD BY THE HONOURABLE HILARY M. WESTON

AWARD WINNER

THE CARDBOARD SHACK BENEATH THE BRIDGE
WRITTEN & ILLUSTRATED BY TIM HUFF

Compassion Series **BOOK 2**

FOREWORD BY THE HONOURABLE DAVID C. ONLEY

IT'S HARD NOT TO STARE

HELPING CHILDREN UNDERSTAND DISABILITIES

WRITTEN & ILLUSTRATED BY TIM HUFF
PARENT & TEACHER DISCUSSION GUIDE BY JAN FUKUMOTO

Forewords by Ray Aldred and Steve Bell

Parent and Teacher Discussion Guide Included

Sharing the Beauty of Canada's Indigenous People with Children, Families and Classrooms.

the HONOUR drum
WRITTEN BY CHERYL BEAR AND TIM HUFF
PARENT AND TEACHER DISCUSSION GUIDE BY CHERYL BEAR
ILLUSTRATED BY TIM HUFF

AM I SAFE?

Exploring Fear and Anxiety with Children

Includes a Discussion and Activity Guide, and a special feature from singer/songwriter Steve Bell

WRITTEN BY IONA SNAIR AND TIM HUFF
ILLUSTRATED BY TIM HUFF

MAKE WAY FOR THE Christmas HUSH

WRITTEN AND ILLUSTRATED BY TIM HUFF

THE JELLYBEAN KID

A tender family-friendly story about a young boy's difficult health journey

INCLUDES a guide to support families with children experiencing critical or chronic illnesses

WRITTEN BY TIM HUFF AND MARGIE TIMPSON
ILLUSTRATED BY TIM HUFF

Find all of Tim's books for kids, teenagers and adults as well as audio books at
compassionseries.com/books.

www.ingramcontent.com/pod-product-compliance
Lightning Source LLC
Chambersburg PA
CBHW040853100426
42813CB00015B/2790

9 781998 815128